CW00557023

I asked God that question too

This work is dedicated to Mama and Papa Wu who gave me the freedom to know God.

I asked God that question too

**Illustrated parables
by
Wuzzy Wu**

f r a m e w o r k s

FRAMEWORKS
38 De Montfort Street, Leicester LE1 7GP,
England

© Wuzzy Wu, 1990

All rights reserved. No part of this publication
may be reproduced, stored in a retrieval
system, or transmitted, in any form or by any
means, electronic, mechanical, photocopying,
recording or otherwise, without the prior
permission of the publisher or the Copyright
Licensing Agency.

Unless otherwise stated, Scripture quotations
in this publication are from the Holy Bible,
New International Version. Copyright © 1973,
1978, 1984 International Bible Society.
Published in Great Britain by Hodder and
Stoughton Ltd.

First published 1990

**British Library Cataloguing in Publication
Data**
Wu, Wuzzy, *1963–*
   I asked God that question too.
   1. Christian life
   I. Title
   248.4

   ISBN 0–85111–212–9

Set in Palatino 14/17
Typeset in Great Britain by Input Typesetting
Ltd, London
Printed in Great Britain by Cox & Wyman Ltd,
Reading

*Frameworks is an imprint of Inter-Varsity Press,
the book-publishing division of the Universities and
Colleges Christian Fellowship.*

Contents

CHAPTER ONE

Why did God make up rules?

Rules hold me back,
stifle my creativity, oppress
my imagination.

I feel so confined and
shackled,
like a netted butterfly,
like a whale in a pool.
I feel locked up.

The fence seems infinite.
I have had it.

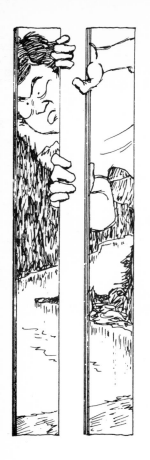

I am going to break free;
rebel against 'what has
always been',
free myself from these
dictatorships.

Don't tell me what to do.

The more I struggle, the
worse I become.
Too frustrated to fight.
My anger turns inward.

Then God's love and concern
showed me a vision and
revealed the truth.

I am standing outside the fence.

My eyes are opened. My mind understands.

Rules are like fences. They simply guide you away from hazards, just as God's laws guide us away from spiritual and physical harm.

'As the Father has loved me, so have I loved you. Now remain in my love. If you obey my commands, you will remain in my love, just as I have obeyed my Father's commands and remain in his love. I have told you this so that my joy may be in you and that your joy may be complete.'

John 15:9–11

CHAPTER TWO

'How can a mortal be holy?'

In our kitchen, there is a set of knives. My mother acquired them for preparing food. There is a bread knife, a paring knife, a meat cleaver and a genuine 'Gourmet Chef's Knife'.

On occasion, my dad will borrow the bread knife to trim his exotic plants. A branch here, a twig there – my dad has many plants.

On occasion, my brother will borrow the paring knife to carve off the rough edges of his wooden, model ships. A sliver here, a shaving there – my brother has many model ships.

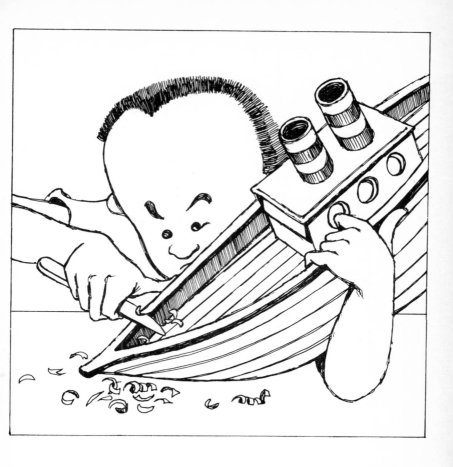

On occasion, I will borrow
the meat cleaver (a stubborn
lid on an old can of paint
quickly yields its grip to the
solid blade of a meat cleaver).
A jiggle here, a pry there –
I have many cans of paint.

Every day, my mother prepares our family meal. She dices and slices vegetables and meats with her genuine 'Gourmet Chef's Knife'. A chop here, a slice there – my mother prepares the best meals.

The 'Gourmet Chef's Knife' is mum's most reliable knife. Since its creation, it has been reserved for preparing mum's gourmet masterpieces. It is regularly fine-honed against a sharpening steel and always placed back into its storage block until it's called upon again.

In our kitchen, there is a set of four knives. Each knife was forged and honed into a precision instrument. But, because three of those knives were subjected to abuse, there is only one that can be trusted to perform the task for which it was originally designed – only one knife can be trusted to perform exceptionally and consistently well.

We are like knives, but created with a godly purpose. Our talents are like blades, crafted for holy accomplishments. Talents are to be protected, nurtured and used by God daily.

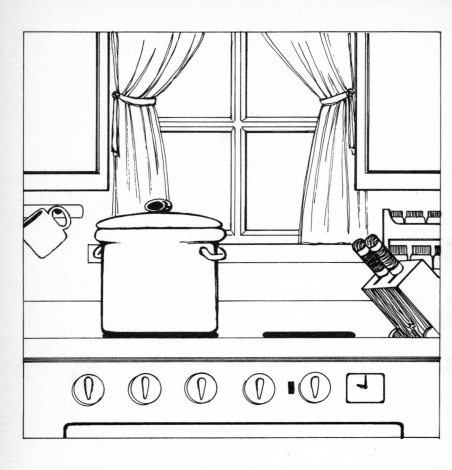

'For we are God's
workmanship, created in
Christ Jesus to do good
works, which God prepared
in advance for us to do.'

Ephesians 2:10

CHAPTER THREE

'Why am I so shallow?'

Why did they laugh, when
they knew I couldn't?
Their laughter made me feel
– different.

If they don't want me,
I'll find others who do.

I don't need them.

Why would they reject me,
when I desperately want
their approval?

If they don't want me,
I can stand alone.

I don't need them.

Some experts told me that I
am most inadequate, but that
they have what I need.

But what they gave me did not satisfy.

I am without hope.

Why is it so impossible for
them to show me kindness?   .

They will never see me weak again. I know how to be strong.

I know how to be strong.

Then the compassionate God
saw me.

I have lived in a land of the self-protected.

I have hidden in my fortress.

So have they.

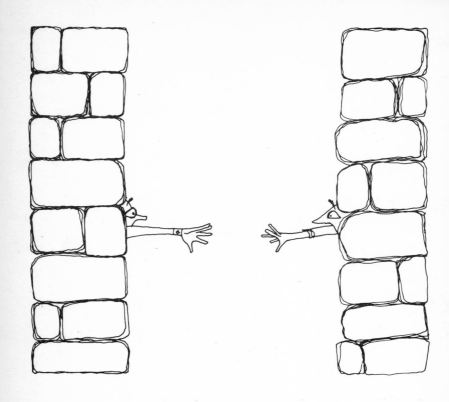

I am restrained by fear.

Jesus,
please help me overcome.

I want to dance in the fields
with the lilies.
And the sky is open for
someone to fly.

I need you.

'Finally, all of you, live in harmony with one another; be sympathetic, love as brothers, be compassionate and humble. Do not repay evil with evil or insult with insult, but with blessing, because to this you were called so that you may inherit a blessing.'

1 Peter 3:8–9

CHAPTER FOUR

'How come life is so complicated?'

I started on a journey to the land of milk and honey. The promised land of my heavenly Father. The place of continuation.

All I needed was provided.
As surely as he fed the
sparrows, the Lord of all
supplied my needs.

I knew my journey would be long, filled with challenge. But 'Praise the Lord', I thought, 'there are ways of making the trip easier.' 'Hallelujah', I thought, 'what a generous God.'

But the pathway to eternity became increasingly tough. My acquisitions soon grew into obligations. My obligations quickly blossomed into debts. The song of joy I once whistled, ceased. I cried in anguish and bondage. I thought, 'This will pass, it has to pass.'

Was there a greater fool than
I, who had traded freedom in
Christ for chains, the lies of
this world?

I was determined to reach the
land, my inheritance, but a
great force held me back.

Jesus, I will look to you.

He has heard my plea.
He has kept his promise.
He has delivered me.

'Do not work for food that spoils, but for food that endures to eternal life, which the Son of Man will give you. On him God the Father has placed his seal of approval.'

John 6:27

CHAPTER FIVE

The Bible – the Word of God

When I read the Word of God, I look on to a glowing horizon.

From out of the darkness there appears a glimmer of hope.

When I meditate on the Word of God, I rise above despair. Its beauty beckons me, its warmth arrests my fears.

When I memorize the Word of God, I soar in truth.

I never dreamed of such power – such attraction.

'Seek the Lord while he may
        be found;
    call on him while he is
        near.
Let the wicked forsake his
    way
    and the evil man his
        thoughts.
Let him turn to the Lord, and
        he will have mercy on
        him,
    and to our God, for he will
        freely pardon.

'For my thoughts are not your
        thoughts,
    neither are your ways my
        ways,'
                declares the Lord.

'As the heavens are higher
    than the earth,
  so are my ways higher than
    your ways
  and my thoughts than your
    thoughts.
As the rain and the snow
  come down from heaven,
and do not return to it
  without watering the earth
and making it bud and
    flourish,
so that it yields seed for the
    sower and bread for the
    eater,
so is my word that goes out
    from my mouth:
  It will not return to me
    empty,
but will accomplish what I
    desire

and achieve the purpose
for which I sent it.
You will go out in joy
and be led forth in
peace;
the mountains and hills
will burst into song before
you,
and all the trees of the field
will clap their hands.
Instead of the thornbush will
grow the pine tree,
and instead of briers the
myrtle will grow.
This will be for the LORD's
renown,
for an everlasting sign,
which will not be
destroyed.'

Isaiah 55:6–13

Close to His Majesty
An invitation to walk with God

DAVID C. NEEDHAM
with Larry Libby

Do you want to know more of God? Do you long to lose yourself in 'wonder, love and praise' as you catch fresh glimpses of his majesty? Then this book is for you.

Sharing insights from his own experience and the Bible, David Needham inspires us not simply to learn about God, but to '*taste* and see that the Lord is good'.

'Readable . . . relevant . . . prophetic . . . leaving you with a sense of God' (from the Foreword by Jim Graham).

240 pages   *Pocketbook*

FRAMEWORKS

The Career Starter Guide
Finding and mastering your
first job
ALAN MacDONALD,
TONY CAMPOLO and others

Rarely is the pressure to conform to the world
harder than when choosing a career path and
starting a new job. This is when our faith really
shows what it is made of.

In *The Career Starter Guide* these challenges are
met head-on in a highly practical handbook for
young adults leaving education and training or
starting a first job.

Priorities, guidance, interviews, applications,
marriage, witness and money are just some of
the key issues tackled.

96 pages   *'B' format*

FRAMEWORKS

The Time of Your Life

ALAN MacDONALD,
TONY CAMPOLO, etc.

When it comes to discipleship, every Christian
wants a truly biblical lifestyle. But for young
adults this involves special dilemmas about
using time and living in the world. Dilemmas
about whether to drink, attend parties or listen
to rock music. How to evaluate films, enjoy
sport and make friends and whether to be
involved in social action.

Here is biblical and practical teaching which
uses full-colour illustrations, personal interest
stories and gifted authors.

96 pages   *Large paperback*

FRAMEWORKS